THE CUSTODIANS

A PLAY IN 3 ACTS

KINGSLEY L. DENNIS

Published by Beautiful Traitor Books – http://www.beautifultraitorbooks.com/

ISBN-13: 978-0-9954817-6-3 (paperback)

First published: April 2016

Cover Concept: Kingsley L Dennis
Cover Design: Ibolya Kapta

Kingsley L Dennis, PhD, is an author and researcher. He currently lives in Andalusia, Spain.

He can be contacted at his personal website: www.kingsleydennis.com

By the same author

The Foundation: The Enigma of a Community

The Citadel: A Mystery at the Heart of Civilization

The Phoenix Generation: A New Era of Connection, Compassion, and Consciousness

Mundus Grundy: Trouble in Grundusland

Meeting Monroe: Conversations with a Man who Came to Earth

Dawn of the Akashic Age: New Consciousness, Quantum Resonance, and the Future of the World (co-authored with Ervin Laszlo)

Breaking the Spell: An Exploration of Human Perception

New Revolutions for a Small Planet

The Struggle for Your Mind: Conscious Evolution & The Battle to Control How We Think

The New Science & Spirituality Reader (co-edited with Ervin Laszlo)

New Consciousness for a New World

After the Car (co-authored with John Urry)

THE PLAYERS

Anwar the Custodian - About fifty years old. Is of medium height, is lean and of average appearance. He has long hair and a long beard that is still dark brown and not yet aged. In fact, he looks rather youthful for his years. He wears a white tunic of woollen appearance and sandals. He gives the image of an ascetic.

Father Nuri - He is an older man of about seventy years of age. He is lean and tall with long scraggy grey hair and a long grey beard. His eyes have an intense and concentrated stare. He too is a custodian of a shrine and was once Anwar's teacher. Like Anwar he wears a white woollen tunic and sandals, which give an overall ascetic appearance.

Nassa - He is a man of about forty years old although his age cannot be exactly verified by his appearance. His hair is short, dark and bushy and shows little sign of ageing. He has a dark moustache which is also bushy and which gives his face a jolly look. He is below average in height and a little chubby. He is dressed casually, with baggy trousers and scruffy shirt half-tucked in underneath a thin jacket.

Young Man - This man is in his middle twenties and is clean-shaven and of respectable appearance. He looks youthful and his light coloured hair, cut very short, is in contrast to the other characters. He speaks with a softer voice.

NOTE ON SETTING

Most of the play takes place within a single location - that of the area in front of the shrine, besides a large tree, with a simple - yet life-size - reed hut in the background. Only one scene (A2, S3) takes place in a different location, this being besides a small stream with a waterfall in the background.

ACT ONE

SCENE ONE

A small white domed tomb (the shrine) can be seen at the back left of the stage. At the back right of the stage stands a life-sized reed hut. At centre-back stands a tall tree with overhanging branches.

The scene begins in the morning sun.

(Anwar walks around from the back of the tomb to the front. He has his back to the audience – pauses – then turns and walks to the tree. He looks up at the tree, then to his left and his right. He stands facing the audience)

Anwar: Signs *(pauses)* Where have all the signs gone? Nowhere to look now. It was easier before *(he walks around the tree)*. Then we had signs – all kinds of signs...especially the ones you couldn't really see. But men, our men, are confusing us with all their new worlds. Where's the distinction in that? They come with their imagined ideas, what is what and what it isn't – but they're only seeing what they want to see. In the end it all comes from them; then they claim it as reality. I mean, where is the reality in all that?
(He sits down under the tree in a cross-legged position – pauses – then hangs his head in contemplation – then raises it again)

Many of them have passed here…they come to visit…some on pilgrimages, others just travellers on the road. When they see the shrine they all beg for a blessing – "Some baraka for our journey" – they say with pious faces *(looks over at shrine – points and nods)*. They all see that – "Such a wonderful shrine – must have been such a saintly man" they say – "one of the Lord's true friends". Well, they do give more when they imagine the blessing to be greater. For the love of heaven and reward…that's the lot of them nowadays. Not much in the middle – purgatory just doesn't pay *(looks up at the tree again)*. Can good fruit come from a bad tree? Grafting new fruit onto it will come to no good…no, the tree must be planted anew, from the bottom up before any good can come from it again *(he stands up and begins to pace around the front of the tree, looking up at the sky and out at the audience)*…lots of the blue stuff up there…like a picture really…it's like I'm living in a picture…but nowadays I'm using more words than I used to. Yes – that's it! The signs have become mere words! *(he begins to pace back and forth along the stage as if in thought)* The words don't read anymore – just silhouettes to a lost cause. I sit here day after day…longing for something that…*(pause)* …that…well…I was sure what it was once; I was even on the way to having it…but then the signs stopped being clear – things became vague *(he goes over to the tomb and begins to shake his head. He returns to the tree again and sits down. He drops his head as if in a state of deep contemplation)*

Father Nuri enters the stage slowly from front right. He stands still looking over at the shrine.

Father Nuri: Ah, I see. The shrine stands before me – I have arrived. Yet who may this well-known custodian be? People speak well of him; speak of his piety and austerity. They say his faith and devotion is strong. This custodian must surely be a holy man – holier than even myself *(Father Nuri approaches the shrine)* Greetings to the Holy One, guardian and protector of the shrine *(he hails Anwar with a raised hand)*

Anwar: *(looks up from his contemplation)* Greetings, traveller. Welcome to this Abode of Spring.

Father Nuri: May you be favoured in the eyes and heart of our Lord.

Anwar: May your coming be auspicious.

Father Nuri sits down near to Anwar. Both men eye each other – then they simultaneously show shock and surprise.

Anwar: Can it be? Is this the face of my old teacher, the one who became as my own father? *(Anwar reaches over and kisses Father Nuri's hand)*

Father Nuri: Anwar, my son! By the Lord's favour it is auspicious indeed that I find you here as custodian of this shrine. I have travelled far, although not in expectation of ever finding thee.

Anwar: Ah, Father Nuri – my teacher and guide – what great event has brought us together like this?

Father Nuri: The question is – what brought you here to be custodian of this shrine? I still remember the day you parted from me.

Anwar: Father – it is events too unclear to be clear of, the truth of which I am unsure.

Father Nuri: It seems that the reason you are here is because of me, and the reason for my being here is because of you. *(Both men simultaneously lean their heads forward to take a moment of reflection, then lift them again at the same time)*

Anwar: Explain, Father. I appear to find myself at a slight loss of inspiration behind the wisdom of your veiled words.

Father Nuri: You see, my son – *pauses* – you are here because I dismissed you from my service.

Anwar: Yes, how I remember those immortal words: "Anwar, my son, it is time to dismiss you from my service. Be gone"

Father Nuri: Ah, it was so, it was so, my son. And such words were carefully chosen.

Anwar: How so?

Father Nuri: With thought.

Anwar: Yes, I suspected as much.

Father Nuri: But let us reach the kernel of our reason.

Anwar: Go on, Father, do not be interrupted.

Father Nuri: You had been my most faithful disciple.

Anwar: The only one.

Father Nuri: *(looks at Anwar curtly)* You stayed with me for near thirty years. You cared for my needs and did great service for our shrine.

Anwar: Yes, those near thirty years are still dear to my heart. I learnt much from your austere company, Holy Father.

Father Nuri: May our Lord look favourably upon his humble servants.

Anwar/Father Nuri: *(in chorus)* Amen!

Father Nuri: I sent you away, Anwar, because it was time for your own service to commence. You had learnt well the humility of service to your teacher – it was time you experienced the world and gave your service to humanity. Thus did it pass.

Anwar: Ay, it was an unforgettable occasion…the day we parted company - you the elder, me the younger *(Father Nuri nods wisely)* I set off from your blessed and bountiful shrine in order to traverse the seas of my own destiny.

Father Nuri: *(puzzled)* But you came by donkey, didn't you?

Anwar: Oh, most assuredly so, Father. By the same donkey donated by your very hand.

Father Nuri: Kindly supplied by a rich pilgrim traveller.

Anwar: So it was.

Father Nuri: And fate no doubt was the very donkey that brought you to this shrine?

Anwar: Oh, that is the very truth of it – if only you knew.

Father Nuri: I know Fate well. And did you not leave the donkey at the door when you stepped into this new house of our Lord?

Anwar: Again, the very truth of it – how well you know.

Father Nuri: I know Fate well.

Anwar: I understand now that I am truly here because of you. Yet please enlighten my darkened mind on how it is that you find yourself here because of me.

Father Nuri: Anwar, my son, the roads that one must travel are of many paths.

Anwar: With many crossroads, my Holy Father.

Father Nuri: *(looks oddly at Anwar)* Yes, with those too.

Anwar: And which road did your holy feet take to bring you here into my humbled presence?

Father Nuri: *(pointing behind him)* The one over yonder.

Anwar: *(nodding)* Most wise...and the seed of your visit?

Father Nuri: *(puzzled)* The kernel of our reason?

Anwar: The grape of our wine, the drops of our ocean...

Father Nuri: *(interrupting)* Yes, yes, I'm coming to that, my patient Anwar.

Anwar: *(placing his hand upon his heart)* With your blessing

Father Nuri: The decree that brings me here is the magnanimity of your popularity. You have, with our Lord's favour, gained such a high degree of sanctity amongst the common people that all speak of your shrine. Pilgrims, merchants, travellers...all those who are to undertake a task first seek favour and blessing from this very shrine.

Anwar: I believe it is so, Father – they all come regularly now.

Father Nuri: I fear so.

Anwar: Fear?

Father Nuri: *(becomes sullen)* The rivers of our protectors have dried up to our old shrine. No longer do they come to seek blessing from where I sit. Now they all take the road to your shrine.

Anwar: I see. Yet the Lord is our true protector is He not?

Father Nuri: The Lord is the Protector of all creation.

Anwar/Father Nuri: *(in chorus)* Amen!

Father Nuri: Yet he doesn't leave food like he used to. With the visitors no longer coming, gifts of food are no longer left for me.

Anwar: This is indeed tragic…a sign of things to come.

Father Nuri: So I resolved to set out to visit the custodian of this new shrine - to bear witness to the magnificence of my competitor.

Anwar: I see *(falls silent)*…Would you like some fruit and nuts?

Father Nuri: *(face brightens)* Oh yes, I'm starving!

Anwar stands and goes into the hut behind. After a pause Father Nuri stands and follows.

****

SCENE TWO

It is early afternoon. Anwar and Father Nuri are sitting under the tree in meditation. A scruffy man appears at the right side of the stage. He looks around searchingly, and then nods his head approvingly. On seeing the two men in meditation he smiles and approaches them. They do not register his presence. He stands next to them, facing the auditorium.

Nassa: *(speaks to audience)* They seem to be…meditating. What a fine hobby. I wonder what they're thinking of? It can't be much fun without a television around here. Perhaps they're wishing that they had a car so they could drive into the nearby town to pick up supplies. I guess telephoning is out of the question…

Anwar: *(opening his eyes)* The Lord does not require a telephone.

Nassa: *(smiling)* To be sure, honoured sir. What would I know about the qualities of the Lord? I'm just a poor, simple man.

Anwar: True, yet let us not dwell upon our chosen roles. Welcome to this Abode of Spring. May your coming be auspicious.

Nassa: *(saluting)* And may your belly be always full.

Anwar: Half-full.

Nassa: Half-full, venerable sir. Unfortunately, being a poor, simple man I have no gifts to offer the custodian of this shrine. I have only myself.

Anwar: And who is myself?

Nassa: *(grinning)* It is Nassa – he who possesses nothing and is himself not possessed *(again he bows)*.

Anwar: And does our brother Nassa have any redeeming qualities?

Nassa: There are those who say I have...*(pauses)*

Anwar: Come now, speak. It is no infliction to be among those of the common man. Our Lord has great use of such hands of labour...*(pause)*...even if such hands commit acts of sin *(he raises a questioning brow)*

Nassa: *(shifting his feet suspiciously and looking around)* Erhh...

Anwar: *(nodding his head and smiling piously)* Drink, is it? Do you come here to seek blessing for an alcohol related problem?

Nassa: *(shaking head slowly)* No...

Anwar: Psychological imbalance of the left and right hemispheres perhaps?

Nassa: *(touching his head)* No...

Anwar: Marital misdemeanours? A man who slaps his wife?

Nassa: *(shaking his head violently)* Oh no!

Anwar: A pinch of adultery? Or weakness in the presence of young ripe flesh when your wife is shrivelled and dry? It's not the greatest sin...many strong men have succumb under strain to the bed of a fair maiden.

Nassa: *(puzzled)* Maiden?

Anwar: *(shrugging shoulders)* Well, it sounds better.

Nassa: Oh, I see

Anwar: No?

Nassa: Oh no, none of these *(looks around the place)*

Anwar: I see now…*(speaking to himself)* A mysterious peddler here, courting mystique through devious denial.

Nassa: What's that?

Anwar: I said you are a mysterious brother indeed – for one so short, you inspire high curiosity. Anyway, your travelling here is the effort required to gain acceptance for a blessing. The shrine is over there *(points with thumb)*…please don't pray too loud, we're meditating. You'd be surprised how noisy some people's ecstasy is nowadays.

Nassa: *(walks over to the shrine, taps it and listens. He walks around the shrine looking unimpressed)* Mmm… *(pause)* … mmm … mmm … *(He scratches his chin several times)* … mmm …

Father Nuri: *(opening his eyes for the first time)* What's all this umming about?

Anwar: *(nodding to where Nassa is standing)* It's the new chap. He's an odd one – a perplexing creature. He doesn't seem to be aware of his own faults.

Father Nuri: Mmmm … mmm … I see *(scratches his chin-beard)*

Anwar: Obviously not one blessed with inner perception.

Father Nuri: Does not remember himself, no doubt. What's his name?

Anwar: Oh *(pause)* … I forget.

Father Nuri: Mmm, I see. His name itself is not memorable. No doubt he is a man in denial of his own identity. He'll need a thousand blessings before he finds the straight path.

Anwar: He says he's a poor, simple man with no gifts for our shrine.

Father Nuri: Then perhaps just a couple of straightforward blessings will do – the Lord will provide the rest for those less fortunate.

Anwar/Father Nuri: *(in chorus)* Amen!

Nassa: *(strolling back to where the two men are sitting)* Nice shrine there. Why are all those bits of ribbon tied to it?

Anwar: Those are for the prayers of the pilgrims. They ask the saint of the shrine to hear their sincere prayers and to bless them divine favour.

Nassa: Divine favour?

Anwar: Yes – to intercede on their behalf with the Lord.

Nassa: Wow, that's a big undertaking. No wonder the poor man's dead… I presume it's a man?

Anwar: *(vaguely)* I didn't check *(Father Nuri and Nassa both look puzzled)*. Anyhow, those who leave gifts may make a request.

Nassa: Actually, it was you I came to see.

Anwar: *(surprised)* Me?

Nassa: Yes. I am here because of you. And it's probably Divine justice that you are here for me.

Anwar: How's that?

Nassa: I have a question.

Anwar: Is that all?

Nassa: That's all

Anwar: And so what may be the seed of your thought; the kernel of your reasoning; the grape of your consideration? *(Nassa looks confused)* The question! *(in an abrupt manner)*

Nassa: Oh…right…well…what I wanted to ask is whether it is right for such a poor, simple man like myself to allow the Lord's creatures to save my life.

Father Nuri: *(his ears pricking up)* Save your life? The Lord's creatures?

Nassa: Well, I must confess I was deeply impressed and grateful at the time of the experience.

Father Nuri: What experience?

Nassa: Oh…a fish saved my life.

Father Nuri/Anwar: *(in chorus)* A fish saved your life!

Nassa: That's the truth of it. *(Both Father Nuri and Anwar stand up and embrace Nassa)*

Anwar: Oh wonder of the heavens!

Father Nuri: The Seal of Solomon!

Anwar: Solomon of the Solomons! *(Father Nuri looks at Anwar oddly)*

Father Nuri: Holy collaborator with the creatures of our world – we are humble before thee! *(Father Nuri bows and Anwar follows)*

Anwar: This is incredible…extraordinary.

Father Nuri: I have been meditating for fifty years; I have been a seeker on this path for half a century and yet I have never reached such heights of enlightenment…to be given such grace by our Lord's creatures.

Anwar: Surely you are a man blessed.

Father Nuri: And surely it is Fate that brings you here – to humble us with your spiritual blessing.

Anwar: Yes, in fact it is us who are blessed! The Lord has directed this man to us.

Father Nuri: Indeed – it is so! The Lord has recognised our struggle through the temptations of this world…our battle against our carnal selves…

Anwar: Yes! We have fought hard for many years against greed, vanity, and pride, in order to reach our present state of humility.

Father Nuri: And in the knowledge of our sacrifices the Lord brings such a blessed man into our presence.

Nassa: *(smiling)* So it's okay then?

Anwar: Okay?!

Father Nuri: How the man does understate himself!

Anwar: It's divinely inspired! You must teach us how we can also confer with the world's creatures.

Father Nuri: Yes, like our great hero Solomon the Wise.

Anwar: *(pointing at Nassa)* And now like our Brother Nassa.

Father Nuri: Of course, of course… sit brother…open your secrets to the long-suffering custodians of the shrines.

They all sit

Nassa: Sure…but first I'd like to spend some time in meditation with you; perhaps I may be able to learn something from the wisdom of your ways *(both Anwar and Father Nuri seem delighted – they look at each other with beaming faces)*

Anwar: Of course, brother.

Father Nuri: Certainly, Brother Nassa – be amongst us.

Anwar: Sit with us. Bless our humble shrine…let us meditate.

Father Nuri: And may the Lord look down upon us as his worthy subjects.

Anwar/Father Nuri: *(in chorus)* Amen!

****

SCENE THREE

The three men are sitting meditating underneath the tree, with eyes closed. It is early evening; the light is beginning to fade.

Nassa: *(opens eyes)* Ahh!…*(looks around smiling)*… that was enjoyable.

Anwar: *(opens eyes)* What is that, brother?

Nassa: I said it was enjoyable; meditation really calms a person and allows the thoughts to have their own merry little dance.

Father Nuri: *(opens eyes and turns to Anwar)* What's going on – meditation time finished already?

Anwar: Our esteemed Brother Nassa is expounding upon the wondrous benefits of meditation.

Father Nuri: Ah, yes – a time for complete stillness of the mind - where thoughts are frozen and dispelled from their attempts at devious distraction.

Anwar: In complete agreement, Father. It is a time for mending our bodily weaknesses - a time to observe our inner grace and to wonder at the endless complexities of Creation.

Nassa: Well, at least I've figured out what I'm going to do about my neighbour's singing lessons.

Anwar: Disturbing the peace is he?

Nassa: Oh, without a doubt. Every evening after dinner he clears his throat and begins to sing … la le la le la do re mi *(he gives a very bad impression)*

Father Nuri: That sounds terrible!

Nassa: Exactly. My wife is always complaining – says it destroys her peace of mind and makes her angry.

Father Nuri: An angry wife is no good to any man.

Anwar: Indeed so – it breaks a man's inner peace.

Nassa: Been married then?

Father Nuri/Anwar: *(in chorus)* No!

Nassa: Well, my wife is like the devil when she gets angry. Her face puffs up and her tongue is as sharp as a scorpion's sting.

Anwar: So naturally you had to tell you neighbour to stop.

Nassa: Naturally not. Who am I to dictate another man's life? It was far easier for me to join him; and much less painful than my wife's wrath.

Father Nuri: And your dilemma?

Nassa: My newly resolved dilemma was over money. When I went to visit my neighbour to ask for singing lessons I was told that he charged ten pieces of silver for the first lesson, and then five pieces for each lesson after that, on account of the first lesson being the hardest.

Anwar: That's not cheap. In fact, to tell the truth, it's quite expensive.

Nassa: To be sure – yet if I have to pay to escape my wife's anger and her verbal blows, then it must be done.

Father Nuri: And the meditation found this answer for you?

Nassa: It did – and more. It came to me as clear as a misty meadow – *pause (Father Nuri and Anwar wait expectantly)*

Anwar: *(after a long pause)* And?

Nassa: Well, you see, I've decided to ask to start with the second lesson – that way it'll be much cheaper. *(Father Nuri and Anwar nod approvingly)*

Anwar: Our brother here is indeed a man of the spirit.

Father Nuri: And blessed with foresight.

Anwar: And intelligence.

Father Nuri: With such qualities as these, Brother Nassa, you could soon be amongst the elect. Why not throw off your earthly pursuits and devote all your energies to spiritual attainment? The path of servitude and devotion is in need of worthy people like your good self.

Nassa: Could I do it?

Father Nuri: Well, it does require great strength though. It's certainly only for the few. One must overcome all evils.

Nassa: Such as? *(Father Nuri goes silent)*

Anwar: What Father Nuri means is that evils such as women and work are like disease for a spiritual man.

Nassa: I can understand about the wife bit…sometimes…but she can also be a funny old crow. And she can laugh the smelly socks off many a visitor…*(pauses)*…of course, when she's angry, she can sure whip me well.

Anwar: That's what we mean – a wife is a distraction from concentration upon goodness and humility.

Nassa: Living with my wife is a lesson in humility itself.

Anwar: Be that as it may, it isn't the same: true humility needs silence of thought.

Nassa: What about work?

Anwar: The same.

Nassa: The same?

Father Nuri: The same.

Anwar: Yes, the same – it's a distraction. It takes you away from the world of our Lord into the world of earthly illusion. Work is a cruel joke indeed.

Father Nuri: And worldly work shows a loss of faith.

Nassa: How is that?

Father Nuri: *(aside)* Our Brother Nassa may be blessed in some areas but in others he's as thick as my beard!

Anwar: It shows loss of trust in our Lord. To acquire true enlightenment one must place all faith in the protection and providence of our Lord.

Father Nuri: To work is to doubt the Lord's providence, and that is a most heinous error.

Anwar: If the Lord had no wish to provide for his creatures, why would he have created us in the first place?

Nassa: So that we may reach knowledge of him through our own struggles? (*Both Father Nuri and Anwar burst out laughing*)

Father Nuri: You've been listening to his detractors!

Nassa: But how can a person be ready for the spiritual life if his hands do no work for him in this life?

Father Nuri: That age-old heresy...it's just wicked propaganda spread by the land-owning classes to maintain their serf labour.

Anwar: It's the kind of nonsense that the uneducated masses believe in.

Father Nuri: What people need is to return to contemplation of our Lord. Only this will provide salvation on the Day of Judgement.

Nassa: If people didn't work then who would be able to bring you gifts?

Anwar: The Lord will always provide all that we need.

Nassa: Without work, how could the hundreds of thousands of less fortunate people earn their relief?

Anwar: Why concern yourself with such things? There is only the Lord and your relationship with Him.

Father Nuri: Brother Nassa, do you see us worrying? Do we look like men with problems to you? Are we stressed? Do we owe several chickens in debt?

Nassa: I can see not.

Father Nuri: Then, this is the proof of the truth of our spiritual path.

Nassa: But you have none of these problems because you don't live in the world.

Father Nuri: *(opens his hands and raises palms upwards)* Exactly! *(Anwar is smiling and nodding his head in agreement)* Our Lord knows what is best for his humble servants.

Anwar/Father Nuri: *(in chorus)* Amen!

Nassa: *(not looking convinced)* Mmm…but Father, where is the proof of your truth in that?

Father Nuri: If it were not true, it would not be so. *(Father Nuri and Anwar look at each other in broad, self-congratulatory smiles)*

Anwar: And since it is so – evident from us as we sit here – then it naturally follows that it must be true.

Nassa: *(shaking his head whilst grinning)* It seems you have it all wrapped up… although I don't claim to follow your understanding.

Father Nuri: Understanding cannot be given, Brother Nassa – it must be earned, as I have earned it through all my years of sacrifice and austerity.

Anwar: And as I have earned it also through the many years of service at Father Nuri's side - and as I sit here as servant and custodian to this shrine.

Nassa: And what, Brother Anwar, have you come to understand?

Anwar: *(hesitatingly)* Well…it…erh…it cannot easily be given in a few words.

Father Nuri: Or any words.

Anwar: That's right – or any words *(shows a smile of relief)*

Father Nuri: It is an understanding that knows no speech. It is wordless like…like a place where words don't exist.

Anwar: In a wordless universe – speechless! *(Father Nuri looks askew at him)*

Nassa: I can see that I still have much to learn *(Father Nuri and Anwar both nod in agreement)*

Father Nuri: At least Brother Nassa understands that he is a man with faults. This is a good sign.

Anwar: How can a broken thing be repaired if it does not know it is broken? Or a watch - how can a watch be wound if it doesn't realise it needs winding?

Nassa: Aha – so I'm an unwound watch in need of winding!

Father Nuri: Purely figurative metaphysics, my brother. Anwar was charming you with the complexities of his thought. Thank you, Anwar, my son. *(Anwar gives a bow with a hand on his heart and a proud smile on his face)*

Nassa gets up and stretches himself. He strolls around the tree, up and down the stage, marching his legs to get some exercise. This looks quite comical. He then returns to his original spot.

Nassa: *(still standing)* That's better – put some juice back into the old joints. Lubricate the elasticity of the body *(proceeds to bend his knees, crouching to the floor and up again. He does this several times, and then extends his arms. The workout lasts for over a minute. All the time Father Nuri and Anwar are eyeing Nassa suspiciously. Finally he stops and stands still, looking over the auditorium).* So, tell me, brothers of the spiritual path, how is one to get this new understanding?

Anwar: By meditation.

Father Nuri: And sincerity.

Anwar: By sincere meditation

Nassa: *(looks a little disappointed. He stares down at his sitting place, then bends his knees again)* Oh well, here goes…*(he sits down with a grimace)*

All three men close their eyes. Nassa opens his and looks at the other two. He then closes his eyes again.

****

SCENE FOUR

It is night time. The three men are sitting under the stars in the same positions. All three of them have their eyes open and are staring expressionlessly into the auditorium. Father Nuri begins to rub his eyes, Anwar both his ears, and Nassa rests with his hand over his mouth, elbow on knee. They look similar to the three monkeys.

Anwar: Esteemed brother and neophyte upon the Way, are you ready to tell us the secret of your communion with the holy fish?

Nassa: Custodian of the Holy Shrine, I am but a poor and simple man who feels himself spiritually lacking in your presence. Allow me some more time so that I may remain here a little longer.

Father Nuri: Anwar my son, let our brother tarry with us a while. We must first of all prove to our Lord that we are worthy of such secrets. It is evident to me now that Brother Nassa is but an instrument in the Lord's hands. Although he is a man without much spiritual development it is clear that he has been singled out as a carrier of this message.

Anwar: And we have been blessed as the recipients of such knowledge, isn't it so Father?

Father Nuri: It is. So let us not add haste to our spiritual endeavour. Surely we, as patient ones, can wait a little more.

Anwar: Wise Father, let it be so.

Nassa: Custodian, I have a question.

Anwar: Make it be. *(Nassa looks blank)* Offer it brother.

Nassa: Well, it's nothing really. I was just wondering how you yourself came to enter the spiritual path.

Anwar: Ah, that…*(Father Nuri tuts)*…it had to be providence brother, that's the only word for it *(he bows his head in silent thought)*

Father Nuri: A woman broke his heart.

Nassa: Really?

Anwar: *(a little ruffled)* It…it was…yes, to be true…but it was Divine Providence that sent the woman to break my heart.

Nassa: How's that?

Anwar: I consider it a time when I was tempted by the sensual pleasures *(begins to reminisce)*…she was the prettiest girl in the town, by my reckoning. I was infatuated with her and she knew it I suppose. She always allowed me to dote on her, for which I was grateful. I did everything she asked of me.

Nassa: Everything?

Anwar: Oh yes…unfortunately, or fortunately for me now, the only thing she never asked of me was sexual favours.

Nassa: Shame.

Anwar: Mmm…I thought so too at the time.

Nassa: So what happened?

Anwar: It continued like this for months…months. I would come to her house to do her cleaning, to do all her chores…I spent all my savings on buying her beautiful things.

Nassa: And she returned nothing? Not even a kiss?

Anwar: Nothing, brother. She would come and spend hours at my house. Even when I wasn't there she'd patiently wait for my return. I was besotted with her.

Nassa: But nothing?

Anwar: I took it all as a sign of her purity and that she was saving herself for me…for the final time when… *(pauses)*

Nassa: And was she?

Anwar: Was she what?

Nassa: Saving herself for the…final time when? *(Anwar remains silent, distracted)*

Father Nuri: Go on, son, reveal to our brother the salacious bit. There's no real shame in humiliation. *(he turns to Nassa)*...it gets better now *(Father Nuri chuckles to himself)*...my son, reveal to us all how the fleshy disease of desire does make a lavatory out of our bodily hopes.

Anwar: Father, please! Respectfully, I did love this girl.

Father Nuri: But son, she was sleeping with your younger brother! *(chuckles)*

Anwar: *(sulkily)* That was my line! I wanted to tell our brother here of my lady's misguided infidelity.

Father Nuri: *(seriously)* Son, that is your greed and vanity displaying itself. You wanted to tell the whole story only to gain pity and sympathy from our new listener here.

Anwar: *(bows head)* Yes, Father Nuri – once again you are right.

Nassa: *(unsympathetically)* So the dame broke all your heart strings!

Anwar: *(still feeling a bit sulky)* Yeah...I came home early one day and caught her in bed with my younger brother.

Nassa: What did she say?

Anwar: She said it was all my fault. My selfless obsession and constant doting had driven her to seek refuge in another man.

Nassa: So you dropped everything and ran away to the spiritual legion?

Anwar: That's it my friend – that's the way I came to the path.

Father Nuri: And that was how he came to me. He came to my shrine to seek a blessing. I took one look at his wretched condition and instantly knew he was ripe to serve me…I mean…he had all the signs of capacity for spiritual work.

Nassa: Which are?

Father Nuri: *(grinning)* Complete and utter desperation…

Anwar: Father is right. He had to work on me; he taught me that my chief feature was greed.

Nassa: Emotional greed?

Anwar: Greed is everything. It took me many years to learn what true generosity is. Now I understand the need in this world for generosity. It is our duty to strive, without rest, for generosity. We must let the people see that we just want to give to them.

Father Nuri: And may the gracious Lord preserve us in our quest.

Anwar/Father Nuri: *(in chorus)* Amen!

ACT TWO

SCENE ONE

It is morning. The first to appear is Father Nuri. He exits the hut and walks to centre stage. He stretches and looks around, then walks over to the shrine and begins to take some of the ribbons off. Second to appear is Anwar – he exits the hut and comes to centre stage. He stretches also and looks around, same as Father Nuri. He goes over to the shrine and helps Father Nuri take off the ribbons. Last comes Nassa. As soon as he exits the hut he does a loud and exaggerated yawn and also stretches himself. He slowly comes to centre stage and does his knee-bending warming-up exercise. He looks over to Father Nuri and Anwar, who seem not to notice him.

Nassa: *(smiling – to the audience)* I see the spiritual dawn rises early around here. They're hard at work, removing the blessings that people have left. Heavy hands do light work. I wonder if the left hand knows what the right hand does? Well, hand wash hand! The Lord loves him who loves work, especially when it is work on oneself first... but hands are easy to control...after all, what is a hand? A hand by any other name is still a hand...my kingdom for a hand! ...ah, sleep no more, hands do murder sleep...

Anwar: *(calling over)* What is that – do you speak to us, brother?

Nassa: *(smiling broadly)* I said I could murder some more sleep.

Anwar: Brother, sleep is the hand of the devil.

Nassa: Don't I know it! And what do your hands do this morning, holy custodian?

Anwar: My hands are making light work of the task ahead. The blessings must be removed to make room for the new ones.

Nassa: So soon? And what if the blessings have not yet had time to work? *(he taunts Anwar)*

Anwar: They have.

Nassa: And if they have not?

Anwar: If they have not, then they will not.

Nassa: If you can see which blessings have been blessed and which have not, then take the haves and leave the have-nots for a little longer.

Anwar: If the have-nots haven't already, then they will never have.

Nassa: *(laughing)* Your hands are indeed wise, Custodian. My hands are merely limp instruments…and that at best – whereas yours are prophetic seers!

Father Nuri: Brother Nassa, do you toy with my son?

Nassa: Nay, Father, I'm only prodding.

Father Nuri: Well, prod with something lighter – your stick is seemingly heavy.

Nassa: Is my target not worthy?

Father Nuri: Your target is engaged in generous service to the shrine *(Father Nuri leaves the shrine and joins Nassa centre stage)*

Nassa: Of course, how could I forget that our Custodian is striving endlessly for his generosity.

Father Nuri: *(speaking quietly)* Between you and me, brother, our Custodian here has not reached the end of his path.

Nassa: *(conspirationally)* Ah…

Father Nuri: Yes…*(leaning closer to Nassa)*…he's still working on this generosity angle. Best not to push and prod too much…we don't want to upset his fine balance.

Nassa: Of course…

Anwar finishes what he's doing at the shrine and exits the stage.

Father Nuri: My son is quite an emotional man…I recognised it immediately when he first came to me.

Nassa: *(encouraging Father Nuri to continue)* Really? You were quick.

Father Nuri: *(showing his confidence)* Oh yes, I'm happy to say that I caught the bird before it fell from the nest, so to speak.

Nassa: Yes, I see…most important.

Father Nuri: I'm not taking full credit for this, of course – I was, naturally, only the eyes of our Lord.

Nassa: Yes, only the eyes.

Father Nuri: All the same, I could see immediately where our dear brother was failing.

Nassa: And you provided the cure?

Father Nuri: Brother, in this world every man needs a cure.

Nassa: Well said Father.

Father Nuri: For my son here, the cure had to be a cultivation of the spirit of generosity, for he was suffering from selfishness and greed – those were his chief features …*(pauses a moment in reflection, then chuckles)*

Nassa: A memory, Father?

Father Nuri: Yes, yes…I was thinking back *(again chuckles)* to the time when I was with my own teacher. There were four of us then and we all had to name, after our probation period, what our chief feature was.

Nassa: A test?

Father Nuri: Sort of. It was to see if we had penetrated sufficiently to recognise our own faults.

Nassa: Sounds intense.

Father Nuri: Yes, difficult times. Real struggling with oneself it was.

Nassa: Mmm…deep penetration.

Father Nuri: *(Father Nuri nods)* Mmm…we had to go deep down into our very selves – right down to the core y'know. None of this superficial surface stuff done by the imitators today.

Nassa: *(joining in with the nodding)* I can imagine – what did you find?

Father Nuri: The worst of the worst.

Nassa: The worst?

Father Nuri: Vanity! *(Father Nuri spreads open his hands as he says this, to give effect)*

Nassa: Aha!

Father Nuri: Oh yes…mark my words – it was a shocking revelation.

Nassa: But you survived it.

Father Nuri: One had to. There was a circle of us – a halka – and we each in turn had to present our find. My first brother declared that his chief feature was pride; the second that his was over-intellectualisation; the third as dogmatic religiosity…but mine was a true bombshell and the worst of them all.

Nassa: Oh Father, what a burden!

Father Nuri: Ay, it was that; for I had the longest road to travel…my feature of vanity was nothing short of the arse of the devil, my friend.

Nassa: Yes, I see clearly what you mean.

Father Nuri: There was no easy road ahead for me. It's a shock to the seeker's system to recognise that one has the most arduous journey of them all ahead.

Nassa: But journey you must.

Father Nuri: Oh, to be sure…there's no merit in stopping for a roadside picnic on this journey.

Nassa: Such a restful sin.

Father Nuri: *(distractedly)* Yes…well, I believe it's time to gather some fruit and berries for our breakfast *(he looks around for Anwar)* Anwar! *(Anwar enters stage)*

Anwar: Yes, Father?

Father Nuri: I think it's time we collected some breakfast refreshment. Will you assist me?

Anwar: To hear is to obey.

Both Father Nuri and Anwar exit the stage together

Nassa: *(aside)* The journey indeed is a long one – but what companions here! Being so sure of their feet they forgot to look down at the road…

Nassa exits stage in opposite direction to Father Nuri and Anwar.

****

SCENE TWO

A young man in his mid-twenties enters the stage looking lost and frustrated. He is obviously impatient. He goes to the shrine, pauses besides it, then walks over to the hut and peers inside it. He walks over to the other side of the stage – looks blankly out into the auditorium in an expression of confusion – then turns and walks back to the shrine. Kneeling, side-on, he begins to pray. After a short time Father Nuri and Anwar appear on stage lower right carrying a basket of berries between them. Father Nuri holds up his hand to motion to a halt.

Father Nuri: (*quietly*) Look, my son, a pilgrim on the path to redemption. Let us not disturb the solitude of his prayer.

Anwar: He seems in great need: he doesn't even notice our arrival.

Father Nuri: May the saint of the shrine hear his call.

Anwar: May the Lord have mercy upon the soul of the saint of the shrine (*Father Nuri looks oddly at Anwar*)

Father Nuri: Is the saint of the shrine in need of the Lord's blessing also?

Anwar: (*coyly*) It may be so.

Father Nuri: Pray, tell more…who is he that lies buried at our feet and who commands respect from such masses?

Anwar: O beneficial Father, let us not (*is interrupted by the voice of Nassa singing offstage – a non-verbal singing: la de la de da...,etc*)

Nassa: (*appearing on stage*) Oh the beautiful morning is a delightful delight! What glory to have legs that don't ache, eyes that don't blur, a voice that is not lost, and a belly that doesn't mind! (*meanwhile, Father Nuri is trying to shush Nassa with hand gestures, pointing over to where the young man is kneeling. The young man now has his eyes open and is observing the scene*) Ah, a praying man! A new addition to the club.

Young Man: Sir, are you the keeper of the shrine? I am seeking the venerable Custodian.

Nassa: By all degrees I am not – neither a custodian nor venerable. I am Nassa, just a poor, simple man, who possesses nothing and is himself not possessed.

Young Man: Then who may be the one I am seeking?

Anwar: *(coming forward)* Welcome to this Abode of Spring, pilgrim. May your coming be auspicious.

Young Man: Holy sir, I bow to your generosity and pray to your good health.

Anwar: The Lord looks after my health if I do my duty to my fellow men.

Young Man: Then I pray that you may be so kind as to help this poor creature.

Nassa: *(surprised)* Who – me?

Young Man: No, me! I'm the poor one.

Nassa: Oh, right…sorry, continue.

Young Man: *(hesitating as if having lost track of his thoughts)* I mean…well…I need help…I need to find something but I don't know where.

Anwar: *(sympathetically)* Ah, a searcher in need: yes, my son.

Nassa: *(seriously)* What have you lost?

Young Man: Er, nothing…

Nassa: *(interrupting)* Er-nothing?

Anwar: Brother Nassa, let our distressed cousin speak *(gestures to Young Man to continue)*

Young Man: Well, it's not that I've lost something…not really…maybe I had it at one time…but that's not to my knowing…I mean…

Anwar: Young cousin, do not let our rhetorical Brother Nassa confuse you – just get to the point.

Young Man: Yes, of course, holy sir. I am in search of that which will give me the greatest happiness. If I cannot find it my fiancé will not marry me.

Father Nuri: *(walks over after listening to the conversation – he speaks in a matter-of-fact tone)* Pre-marital problems are common in many visitors. Pray before the saint of the shrine, offer a gift, and if your prayer is sincere it will receive a blessing in due time *(he puts his basket of berries on the floor and sits down. Everyone is silent and remains completely still. It is an uncomfortable silence. Father Nuri seems oblivious to this silence)*

Anwar: *(trying to break the silence)* Prayer can work wonders – the truth is revealed only in prayer.

Young Man: But can my truth be found in prayer alone? Will I find the greatest happiness this way?

Anwar: Of course, if it be the Lord's will.

Nassa: Well, well…*(walks up to the shrine and pats it gently)*…happiness is not something that can be given so easily nor asked for so carelessly.

Young Man: So what am I to do?

Nassa: Happiness is to be understood.

Young Man: *(confused)* Am I to offer some gift then?

Anwar: *(quickly)* It might speed things up.

Nassa: Yes, you should offer something. As the saying goes – 'Take what you want says the Lord, but you must pay for it' *(Father Nuri and Anwar are nodding their heads in agreement)*

Young Man: But I only have a little money *(Father Nuri picks up the empty basket and passes it to Anwar, who begins to hold it out)*

Nassa: So you should take what you need by earning the right to take it; and you must pay for it...*(pauses as Anwar offers the basket)*...but not with money *(Father Nuri, Anwar and the Young Man all look at Nassa bewilderedly)*

Anwar/Father Nuri/Young Man: *(in chorus)* Not with money!?

Nassa: *(smiling – obviously enjoying himself)* No – with something more valuable than money...*(pauses)*...with yourself.

Young Man: Myself?

Nassa: Yep – that's the long, short, and bottom of it.

Young Man: But how can I pay with myself? I have nothing to offer?

Nassa: *(still very jovial)* Oh, on the contrary, my brother; you devalue yourself.

Young Man: I do?

Nassa: You do. Everyone has the ability to pay for themselves in this life: unfortunately, so few do.

Young Man: But how?

Nassa: By right living and right thinking.

Young Man: Right living? Right thinking?

Nassa: In not so many words – yes. What is important is how you approach a thing; in this case it's your happiness. If you approach by the wrong means, you'll get something entirely different.

Anwar: *(sounding very sceptical)* And what type of happiness would that be, wise brother?

Nassa: *(turning to Anwar with a grin)* Why, it would be coloured happiness.

Anwar: Erh? Coloured happiness? What, you mean like a red or blue happiness; or perhaps a kind of turquoise happiness with purple edges? *(Anwar is being sarcastic)*

Nassa: Mmm, interesting vision...*(he is unperturbed by Anwar's obvious sarcasm)* What I meant is that the happiness will be coloured by your own prejudices, expectations, and subjectivity. In short, it will be the happiness that you secretly want it to be and not what you need it to be. Ah...*(rubs his hands together)*

Father Nuri: *(grunts)* Sounds like a lot of this new age garbage to me - are you sure you haven't been filling your head with that chemical stuff those long-haired girlie-boys are using? *(Anwar shyly touches his own long hair)*

Nassa: *(laughing)* Oh Father, why would a poor man like Nassa need to indulge his simple mind with such intoxicants?

Father Nuri: Mmm...simple...yes...*(mumbling)*...but I don't see why good old-fashioned prayer isn't good enough for our new friend here. It was good enough for me, Anwar, and all those who came before us.

Anwar: Yes, it's been handed down without even a scratch.

Nassa: Perhaps so – yet what is the worth of prayer without the knowledge of how to ask?

Father Nuri: Brother, don't be superficially deep – anyone can ask.

Anwar: Father Nuri is right, the act of asking isn't difficult.

Nassa: Yet if a donkey prays it still remains a donkey.

Anwar: Brother Nassa! How sinful – what makes you speak like this?

Father Nuri: Our brother here seems to be debasing our holy act of prayer. Does he not realise that I am living proof itself of a life spent in prayer?

Nassa: Transparently so *(bows in respect)*

Father Nuri: So then, why do you speak like this? Your words are inflammatory.

Anwar: Like a flame to cotton!

Father Nuri: Like man's fiery desire for the loins of a woman!

Anwar: Like burning wax on a soft naked body!

Both Father Nuri and Anwar are getting quite worked up now.

Father Nuri: May the Lord protect us in our most needy times.

Anwar/Father Nuri: *(in chorus)* Amen!

Father Nuri and Anwar, feeling relieved once again, sit down on the floor.

Nassa: *(aside – speaking to auditorium)* Wise are the words once spoken – 'Speak to each man in accordance with his understanding' *(turning to Young Man)* Come, you must be hungry. At least accept our hospitality if you cannot fathom our disagreements.

Nassa and the Young Man join Father Nuri and Anwar sitting down. They all become silent and eat their breakfast of berries.

****

SCENE THREE

Nassa and the Young Man are washing their hands and face in a small stream besides a waterfall. They are alone and centre stage.

Young Man: This is a peaceful place.

Nassa: True. It's local name is Abshaur.

Young Man: What does that mean?

Nassa: Waterfall.

Young Man: Ah, logical.

Nassa: Very.

They continue washing

Young Man: Do you know the area around here?

Nassa: Not really.

Young Man: So you're not from around here then?

Nassa: *(smiling)* No.

Young Man: May I ask where you're from?

Nassa: You may

They continue to wash in silence

Young Man: *(after a pause of some time)* Where are you from?

Nassa: Not around here.

Young Man: Oh, I see.

Nassa: Uh huh…

Young Man: *(after another pause of some time)* From where exactly?

Nassa: *(points into the distance)* Somewhere over there.

Young Man: Is it far?

Nassa: Depends on how you travel.

Young Man: I see…*(pause)*…as the bird flies?

Nassa: Then not too far…some people call it Raven's Corner.

Young Man: And you?

Nassa: I just call it home.

Young Man: Yes, logical.

Nassa: Very.

They both stop washing and sit down casually; they both look relaxed. It is a comfortable posture – not a rigid meditative one.

Young Man: Raven's Corner...mmm...never heard of it.

Nassa: It speaks well of you too...Anyway, we don't get many visitors travelling our way.

Young Man: *(trying to be humorous)* Perhaps people don't go there because they're afraid of ravens...*(laughs to himself)*

Nassa: *(very seriously)* No – it's because they don't like corners...

Young Man: Oh...right...*(tries to change the subject)*...do you know why I'm looking for that which will give me the greatest happiness?

Nassa: I don't need to know because you're going to tell me.

Young Man: Well...yes, I guess I am...*(pause)*...It's because I'm in love *(Nassa gives no reaction)*...it's with a woman.

Nassa: Ah, now everything is clear! The woman you love has given you a task to accomplish before she'll consent to marry you.

Young Man: Is it that clear?

Nassa: Like day and night.

Young Man: Y'know, I don't know what to do...she told me that she wouldn't marry me until I had found that which would give me the greatest happiness…and that I was only to return to her when I had found it…*(pause)*… women are strange sometimes…

Nassa: Women are wise sometimes.

Young Man: You think so?

Nassa: I do…yep, I sure do…and it seems to me like you've got one there yourself. Even if you hung her upside-down you'd find more answers between her toes than you'd find here.

Young Man: You think so? *(Nassa nods his head quietly)*. Then why did she set me this task?

Nassa: Have you ever thought about it yourself? *(Young Man nods his head quietly)*…I mean, really thought about it?

Young Man: All the time…night and day.

Nassa: Well, that's a start.

Young Man: Is it a good start?

Nassa: Mmm…do you ever think about what you're doing here?

Young Man: Yes, all the time…*(Nassa slaps his knee)* Owh!

Nassa: That's not what I meant – stop replying without thinking.

Young Man: I wasn't *(Nassa slaps his knee again)* Owh!

Nassa: Have you considered the contribution you can make to the community and people around you? Have you considered your duty in paying back for your existence? And the duty you owe to yourself?

Young Man: *(pauses...hesitates)*...Well....Not really like that, I guess.

Nassa: I guess you haven't.

Young Man: But how does that relate to my fiancé?

Nassa: It doesn't so much relate to your fiancé as to your fiancé's task. A person's happiness will never be complete so long as that person is distracted by every passing thought and each new whim. Such things will blow a person about continuously...

Young Man: *(interrupting)* Like a leaf in the wind?

Nassa: *(looking at Young Man carefully)* Speech has a beginning and an end, so please don't put yours in the middle of mine.

Young Man: *(embarrassed)* Oh...erh...sorry.

Nassa: For many people, happiness depends upon the moment that is passing at that time. Your fiancé understands that marriage should not be from a whim. Hence she's set you a task to question your own happiness until you arrive at a state of objective understanding – not emotive urges. *(there is a long pause)* You can speak now, I've finished.

Young Man: Oh right, thanks...But I still don't understand...how am I to search for this happiness?

Nassa: By asking questions.

Young Man: To whom?

Nassa: To yourself, of course – who else do you think has the answers?

Young Man: The Custodian of the shrine?

Nassa: *(Nassa grins broadly)* There is a saying, my friend – 'You'd ride a donkey to the door but you wouldn't ride it into the house' *(Young Man nods his head but clearly doesn't understand)* Our dear brother the Custodian here is still riding on the back of his donkey. Progress is about adaptation: you wouldn't wear Eskimo furs in the Sahara, would you?

Young Man: I guess not.

Nassa: Today is today and then was then…I hope I have answered your question? *(smiles)*

Young Man: *(looking confused)* Well…erh…

Nassa: Well, 'no' is what you should say.

Young Man: Well, 'no' then.

Nassa: Good.

Young Man: Good?

Nassa: Yes, good – since you like to hear words repeated *(Young Man gives Nassa a funny look)* It all begins by asking yourself the right questions.

Young Man: Is that all?

Nassa: Patience isn't your strongest virtue, is it?

Young Man: I guess not…but that's the way I am.

Nassa: That can soon change. Look – once the right questions get asked to yourself they will begin to penetrate. Then a change will slowly occur. You will have begun the road to waking up.

Young Man: So I'm asleep then?

Nassa: Oh, more than you know it, friend. You're in such a deep sleep that even the Whore of Babylon on discount night couldn't raise you.

Young Man: That bad?

Nassa: It's bad so long as you take your happiness solely from life's circumstances. What you have to find within yourself is that which is the only thing you can take with you from a sinking ship.

Young Man: *(thinking hard)* Mmmm...*(after a while)*...you mean, that's me?

Nassa: In a Greek nutshell, yes.

Young Man: *(claps his hands in joy)* And that's exactly what I'll tell my fiancé! *(Nassa slaps his knee)* Owh!

Nassa: Not so fast, Einstein...what you actually tell your fiancé is that the thing which will bring you the greatest happiness in your life is, of course, her.

Young Man: But why do I have to tell her that...especially after what you've just said?

Nassa: Because you're not planning on spending the rest of your life with me...and if you want a comfortable life then you have to learn the right words.

Young Man: Mm...right words...

Nassa: Besides, it's your duty to make your wife happy even if you're still out there…like your leaf on the wind image.

Young Man: *(smiling proud)* Yes, I kinda liked that image…So, I don't need a blessing from the Custodian then?

Nassa: Nope. But stay awhile longer for their sake.

Young Man: Is it necessary?

Nassa: They require it to feed themselves. Anyway, if you go too soon you'll miss the fireworks.

Young Man: A celebration?

Nassa: A revelation.

****

<u>SCENE FOUR</u>

Both Anwar and Father Nuri are sitting underneath the tree. They are meditating – eyes closed and not speaking. This continues for some time.

Anwar: *(with eyes closed)* There's nothing like meditation, is there Father?

Father Nuri: *(eyes closed)* No.

Anwar: You taught me that.

Father Nuri: I did.

Anwar: So peaceful. No influences from the outside world, no distractions…no disturbances…just silence…peace and quiet.

Father Nuri: Yes.

Anwar: *(opens his eyes)* Father, can I ask you a question?

Father Nuri: *(eyes still closed)* Uh…huh

Anwar: Father *(taps Father Nuri's knees)*

Father Nuri: *(opens eyes)* What?

Anwar: What do you make of our Brother Nassa?

Father Nuri: Strange fellow.

Anwar: I mean, he makes a claim to spiritual attainment…

Father Nuri: He damn near shouted it from the rooftops.

Anwar: Quite so – a bragging fellow…and he makes this claim and yet by all appearances he's just a simple, scruffy man…an odd fellow.

Father Nuri: And dangerous too.

Anwar: Dangerous?

Father Nuri: Yes, I believe this man could be dangerous for us.

Anwar: How so?

Father Nuri: Didn't you see how he behaved with that young man? Telling him that to make an offer of money was not necessary…

Anwar: Ah yes…how could I forget! And the basket was just inches away from him.

Father Nuri: Our odd fellow, Nassa here, may believe that he is a pilgrim on the path to our Lord's love and generosity…but he knows nothing of our Lord's hierarchy.

Anwar: Indeed – so true. Please, go on. I am finding your words like the kernel of great reason, the grape of my wine, like the drop…

Father Nuri: (*interrupting*) Yes, yes, my son…no need to write a play about it.

Anwar: (*hand on heart and bowing*) Of course, my humble apologies.

Father Nuri: If there were no Lord's hierarchy then any old Tom, Harry, and Susan could be proclaiming the Divine message – we must be aware of the false gold.

Anwar: For the false gold has no market value.

Father Nuri: But it does have market value!

Anwar: It does?

Father Nuri: Yes, but only with those who trade in a false market.

Anwar: (*smiling, with pride*) Ah, of course. Yet it is so far from the truth.

Father Nuri: As far from the truth as the bottom of the world is the top.

Anwar: Ostensibly so, Father *(looking a little confused)*

Father Nuri: The Lord's message must be protected from the plebeians and ruffians of this world who would only seek to use it for their own power and privilege.

Anwar: And from those who would seek to escape from the responsibility of payment.

Father Nuri: That is exactly my other point. Is it not wisely written that the Lord once proclaimed - 'Take what you like said the Lord, but you must pay for it'

Anwar: It was - I cannot dispute.

Father Nuri: Indeed you cannot, it would be futile.

Anwar: And do you think our fellow Nassa is one of these redoubtable rapscallions?

Father Nuri: I believe he could be, for it is such people who from mischievous ends wish to deprive the Lord's chosen ones from their rightful duty.

Anwar: *(pausing)* Which is?

Father Nuri: Which is assisting the troubled creatures of this world to offer a sacrifice for their grace. We don't accept any money for ourselves, of course.

Anwar: Of course not!

Father Nuri: The giving of money is a sacrifice demanded by the Lord. You don't get anything for nothing. Our duty is to inspire such sacrifices so that people may obtain their blessings. We must accept our duty with humility.

Anwar: Father Nuri, once again you speak with words that are evidence of your age and wisdom.

Father Nuri: Wisdom that can only be granted by the generous grace of our most magnanimous Lord.

Anwar/Father Nuri: *(in chorus)* Amen!

Father Nuri: And so later let us confront our trickster Nassa and reveal to all the truth behind his false connivance.

Anwar: Let it be so!

ACT THREE

SCENE ONE

Father Nuri and Anwar are both tending to the shrine. Father Nuri looks off-stage and notices something.

Father Nuri: My son, our dubious brother approaches. Follow my behaviour and let us see what mettle our man is made of.

Anwar: My ears hear you.

Nassa and Young Man enter the stage from front left. They are engaged in conversation and walking slowly.

Father Nuri: *(shouts over and approaches Nassa)* Dear Brother Nassa, praise and thanks to our Lord that he has preserved you well and kept your spirit in its majestic home *(Father Nuri kisses Nassa's hand and then gives him a hug – Father Nuri looks over at Anwar)*

Anwar: Dear Brother Nassa, teacher of righteousness, perfected man, where hast thou been? May the Lord ever watch over thy movements *(Anwar comes and kisses Nassa's hand and gives him a hug. The Young Man looks surprised. Nassa looks neither shocked nor surprised – he takes it all calmly, almost seeming to play along)*

Nassa: And may the Lord watch carefully over your movements too, in case you slip.

Father Nuri: *(in a tone of false flattery)* See, Anwar my son, our brother here is indeed a master of high rank; one that not only communes with the Lord's lowly creatures but also strives after our own meek welfare.

Nassa: Is this not the duty of all men?

Father Nuri: It is not brother.

Anwar: It cannot be!

Nassa: Then you sadly neglect the capacity of your fellow men.

Father Nuri: Nay brother, don't speak like an easy optimist. You have the mark of one who lowers himself to serve the low…

Anwar: Then raises himself up to reach the rank of martyr!

Father Nuri: Yes! One who would die for the Lord's people. Is this not so, brother?

Nassa: *(laughs)* I would, venerable sirs – but not as you think. Your words have good appearance yet like an atom are mostly filled with an empty space.

Anwar: Brother, do you deride my teacher?

Nassa: *(waves him away)* I deride no-one.

Anwar: Our Father praises you with such esteemed accolades yet you reward him with insult.

Nassa: I did not come to reward. Besides, he gets enough of that from the many pilgrims who come for blessings.

Anwar: Yet he called you a master of high rank – one who works for all the people.

Nassa: Indeed he did, but what he describes is no more than a normal man.

Father Nuri: *(offended)* A normal man! I did not!

Nassa: What you described were simply the lowest duties of all men: to serve is not to become a saint - it is simply to be human, nothing more.

Father Nuri: Brother, you debase the saints and martyrs of this world.

Nassa: Sir, you debase humankind *(Father Nuri huffs and walks away)*

Father Nuri: *(aside)* He is sneaky, this one…craftier than I first thought. He turns and twists my words as if I am the liar. I do feel he is a threat to us all. Either that or he is a downright dumbo, a certified lunatic.

Anwar: *(turning to Young Man with a smile)* Have you decided to come for your blessing now? Have the rays of our good Lord found their way into your soul?

Young Man: Something is finding its way. I can't quite decide if the rays are penetrating me subtly or boxing the top of my skull.

Anwar: *(fakes a modest laugh)* Ah, how humour takes your tongue!

Young Man: *(seriously)* It wasn't meant to be humorous.

Anwar: *(again faking the same modest laugh)* Don't doubt the mysterious workings of our Lord!

Nassa: Or the banging of common sense *(Anwar frowns at Nassa)* Shall we sit and continue our lively discussion in comfort?

Anwar: *(now less jovial)* Yes, I think it would be a better position for us *(they all sit under the tree – even Father Nuri joins them)*

Young Man: I must admit that I do find it peaceful here. *(Father Nuri and Anwar nod their heads approvingly)*

Nassa: Well, that's partly due to there being no factories, cars, residential areas, air pollution…

Father Nuri: *(interrupting)* Yes, thank you brother – we get the point.

Young Man: I guess it gives ample time for meditation and reflection?

Anwar: There is never enough time for inner reflection upon the Lord's ways. We could live a hundred thousand times over and yet it still wouldn't be enough time to contemplate all the wonders of the universe.

Nassa: *(quietly)* You may have the chance to test your theory.

Anwar: Sorry brother?

Nassa: I said 'May you have the time to contemplate our Lord'.

Anwar: Thank you for your grace *(bowing, yet with eyes looking around distrustfully)*

Nassa: *(with a broad smile)* You're welcome.

Father Nuri: *(with a sweeping hand gesture)* It is the intention of my son Anwar here, and myself, to place the desire of heaven in our hearts now so that we may be prepared for our later entrance.

Anwar: Yes, and to keep the fear of the devil in our hearts also, in order to stay on the path of truth and righteousness.

Nassa: *(shaking his head sadly)* Mm…it is a shame.

Father Nuri: *(obviously offended)* A shame! What do you mean, it's a shame? Do you not understand the true way to good works?

Anwar: Perhaps our Brother Nassa is not such an enlightened man after all? *(gives a conspiratorial smile and nod to Father Nuri)*

Nassa: Ahh…I was thinking back to the stories my mother used to tell *(laughs quietly to himself and begins to rock slowly back and forth)*

Young Man: Yes, what are they? Come on, please do share with us.

Nassa: Oh, it's only a family tale.

Young Man: No, come on Nassa, you mustn't stop now.

Father Nuri: Perhaps our esteemed brother has no real story to tell after all.

Nassa: *(after a pause)* Well…since you all insist. My mother used to tell me about a very old ancestor of ours, who lived many generations ago. Rubya was her name…

Anwar: *(interrupting)* A gem of a lady no doubt! *(he looks around for a response to his joke – there is none)*

Nassa: *(continuing)*…and every night she used to walk around the village with a flaming torch and a bucket of water…

Father Nuri: *(interrupting)* Was she an arsonist with a conscience? *(he too looks for a response – there is none)*

Nassa: *(continuing)*…every night she'd walk around like this and when people asked her the meaning off it, she would reply – 'I've come to burn down heaven and to put out the fires of hell' *(Nassa laughs – both Father Nuri and Anwar look deeply shocked)*

Father Nuri: Oh blasphemy!

Anwar: Jesus Christ! *(Father Nuri slaps him)* Owh!

Father Nuri: She was mad, clearly deranged.

Nassa: Oh yes, I know – completely sane. My mother would call her the wisest of our family.

Father Nuri: Then your family is clearly a loony one – candidates for the state mad house.

Anwar: In need of electro-shock therapy I say *(looks to Father Nuri for approval)*

Father Nuri: *(nodding profusely)* More likely in need of a lobotomy…I was right, he's not a devious trickster but a certified fool – an idiot from an idiotic family. Now it's as clear to me as the crystal gates of heaven. We're saved, he's no threat to us at all!

Young Man: Nassa, was this Rubya truly mad? Is there not an explanation for this?

Nassa: *(unperturbed by the fuss)* Of course. There's a meaning for those who wish to enquire further.

Young Man: Which is?

Father Nuri: Bah, this is nonsense! Our Brother Nassa here is just a nobody…a wannabe, flaunting himself like some false fakir.

Anwar: His pedigree is indeed with the animals who he claims to have saved his life!

Nassa: It was only the fish which saved my life, don't forget.

Father Nuri: Forget! How could we forget? We've been waiting to hear your account of this incredible tale which you've been keeping from us.

Nassa: It is no secret.

Father Nuri: Then reveal!

Anwar: Yes, tell us, go on!

Young Man: Wait! First I want to know the explanation about Rubya.

Father Nuri: Bah!

Nassa: *(very calmly)* I will answer both of your requests. First, I shall satisfy this young man here with Rubya's tale.

Father Nuri: With a Rubya gone mad!

Nassa: On being questioned further, Rubya would reply that…

Anwar: *(interrupting)* That she was a loony! *(both Anwar and Father Nuri laugh together and slap hands)*

Young Man: Honourable sirs, please! Remember that speech has both a beginning and an end, so kindly don't place your heckles in the middle *(Anwar and Father Nuri become sullen like little boys)*

Nassa: Rubya's reply was a simple prayer. She said – 'O Lord, if I worship you from desire of Paradise, deny me Paradise; and if I worship you from fear of Hell, then throw me into Hell' *(all the men become silent)*

Young Man: And so why the torch and water? I still don't understand.

Nassa: By removing the two obstacles of people's false attachment she was opening the way to true worship.

Anwar: True worship being, o brother?

Nassa: It being worship for the sake of service. No other. Not from fear nor desire.

Father Nuri: But these are what people need to motivate them.

Nassa: Exactly.

Father Nuri: Ah, what nonsense! You are truly a muck-raker born of a muck-raker's family.

Young Man: What an insult!

Nassa: On the contrary – I'm pleased to be reminded of my physical origins *(stands up to leave)*

Father Nuri: Not so fast, ex-brother – you haven't yet told us of how a fish once saved your life.

Nassa: Oh, that's easy. I was once wandering for three days without having eaten any food. I was starving. I eventually managed to catch a fish from the river and ate it – I believed it saved my life! *(smiles)*

Father Nuri: *(standing up)* Aha! A true fraudster indeed! At last the truth is known – you're a fake, a charlatan, a...a ...

Anwar: *(standing up)* A cheat and a trickster...

Father Nuri: Yes, yes, yes...a loony...a wacko...a defiler of all things sacred. Be gone from here before we...we...

Anwar: You cheated us! Yes, be gone...there is no room at the shrine for hypocrisy!

Nassa: Indeed there is not *(Nassa continues to speak very calmly)* I will bid you gentlemen farewell for now *(turning to Young Man, who is standing up now)* I hope that your heart will learn to distinguish the false from the real *(Nassa bows and exits the stage)*

Father Nuri: By the grace of our Lord, what a crazy man.

Anwar: Thank the Lord we were able to perceive his falseness before it was too late.

Father Nuri: May the Lord always look after his own.

Anwar/Father Nuri: *(in chorus)* Amen!

Young Man: I quite liked the chap actually *(Father Nuri and Anwar give Young Man a look of surprise and shake their heads)*

All three men sit down again under the tree.

****

SCENE TWO

It is sunset and as the evening is approaching the three men – Father Nuri, Anwar, and Young Man – sit together under the tree sharing a meal of bread and fruit.

Father Nuri: Young man, you were right to want to spend the evening with us; for although you have little to offer, we realise that it is our duty to set you on the straight path.

Anwar: Yes, especially since the disruption caused by that dog Nassa…and to think that we offered him our respect and hospitality.

Father Nuri: It was our hospitality that we extended – the outward displays of respect that we showed to him were merely the required rituals.

Young Man: I see. And so you never really believed that this brother of yours was a spiritual man?

Father Nuri and Anwar look at each other, then burst out laughing.

Father Nuri: What! This man who ate a fish and claimed communion with the animals – it's absurd!

Anwar: If we had been fooled then we would've been sitting at his feet. Did you see us sitting at his feet?

Young Man: Well, not whilst I was…

Anwar: *(interrupting)* You see, there's the proof.

Father Nuri: Done and sealed. Now, come on, no more talk of this foolish man. Let us turn our thoughts to real things.

Anwar: A life spent in triviality is no life at all.

Father Nuri: *(looking at Anwar)* Wasn't that one of my sayings?

Anwar: *(sheepishly)* It was, erh, I believe.

Father Nuri: Bravo my son, you speak well *(Anwar brightens up)*. Now young man, about this problem of yours.

Young Man: My happiness?

Father Nuri: Yes, that's it, your happiness. What do you propose to do about it?

Young Man: Er...well...I don't know really...Nassa said that...

Father Nuri: Nassa was a baboon!

Anwar: An oink!

Father Nuri: Forget the words of braggarts and sons of donkeys. Listen, a wise man once said...I don't remember who, but he was certainly wise because he said – 'A donkey eats rice, meat, and melon, and it remains a donkey'.

Anwar: *(claps his hands in joy)* Bravo!

Young Man: And what does that mean?

Father Nuri: Mean? What does it mean? Don't be so shallow - use your thinking capacity, young man! *(Young Man looks* *blank – there is a silence).* It means that just because an animal behaves like a human being, it doesn't make it one.

Young Man: Ohh…I see… *(seemingly unimpressed)*

Anwar: What our learned Father is trying to convey to you is that this material world of ours is full of false prophets and those that aim to confuse you and lead you astray.

Father Nuri: Many people will pretend to be what they are not. Let those fakers be as mirrors to reflect to the faithful how not to be.

Anwar: We need the fools to teach us. Father, who was it that said – 'Every wise man understands a fool for he himself was once a fool, yet no fool shall ever understand a wise man for he is himself still a fool'?

Father Nuri: A very wise man.

Anwar: Indeed…without a kernel of a doubt.

Father Nuri: Without an ocean of disbelief.

Anwar: Without a cloud of unknowing.

Father Nuri: May the Lord in his wisdom give us strength to endure the ignorant and foolish.

Anwar/Father Nuri: *(in chorus)* Amen!

Both Father Nuri and Anwar appear to be congratulating themselves and not aware of the Young Man's presence.

Young Man: Er, excuse me?

Anwar: Yes?

Young Man: And what about my problem?

Anwar: You still have a problem?

Young Man: Well yes, I think so.

Father Nuri: Haven't we already answered it for you?

Young Man: No.

Anwar: No!? *(astonished)*

Father Nuri: Then what have you been doing?

Young Man: When?

Father Nuri: Now, young man – now!?

Young Man: Well, er…I was…

Father Nuri: *(interrupting)* You were not listening to us, that's what you were doing.

Anwar: How can you expect to learn anything if you don't listen?

Young Man: *(protesting)* I was listening…

Anwar: *(interrupting)* Don't doubt us now.

Young Man: I'm not.

Anwar: It doesn't seem like that to me.

Young Man: I wasn't.

Father Nuri: And ungrateful. After all the words of wisdom we've given to you. Don't you remember anything?

Young Man: *(confused)* Yes, of course I do...the donkey eating a meal...a donkey who eats is still not human...er *(Young Man is obviously thinking hard)*

Anwar: Is that it?

Young Man: Wait...there's erh...fools and mirrors – they'll never be wise cause they're not wise yet...but wise men can be better mirrors to the false prophets...and, er... everything gets reflected back to us to show us our faith...and it's all the kernel of the ocean of unknowing...

Father Nuri: *(shouting)* Masturbation! *(Anwar and Young Man are shocked and become silent).* This is enough! You are masturbating with such sacred words of wisdom. It is an affront.

Anwar: *(reclaiming his composure)* An insult – how dare you!

Young Man: *(stammering)* I...er...didn't mean to, er...it was nothing...

Father Nuri: *(shouting even louder)* Nothing! Nothing! A crime against our Creator. You betray us!

Anwar: You have wounded us!

Young Man: But what?

Father Nuri: *(standing up)* Judas! You betray us by throwing our goodness back in our faces whilst bleating like a lamb. *(Young Man gets up and slowly backs away)* It is worse than Judas's kiss!

Anwar: *(also standing up)* Don't come all innocent with us now – your true face has shown itself.

Young Man: *(nervously)* What face?

Father Nuri: You come as a beggar and yet you came to steal. Get thee behind me Satan!

Anwar: And thee behind me too! *(Young Man backs away further)*

Father Nuri: That's right, try to escape when the true colours are called.

Anwar: When the flag is flying you cannot deny the presence of the wind!

Young Man: *(backs off towards the stage exit)* What? I don't understand…I…I feel utterly humiliated…

Father Nuri: Be gone, usurper!

Anwar: Flee like a coward before our Lord.

Young Man exits. Father Nuri and Anwar remain standing for a while, then return to their sitting position.

Father Nuri: There goes another. They always try it on.

Anwar: They come meekly but soon disappear with their tales between their legs.

Father Nuri: Betrayers.

Anwar: Losers.

Father Nuri: It is good that we remain ever vigilant and strong in our faith.

Anwar: It is indeed. The Lord does test us.

Father Nuri: Oh, how true. The Lord in his infinite wisdom sends down to us trials and tribulations in which to test our devotion.

Anwar: And yet we always come through.

Father Nuri: To which we must give praise and thanks to our Lord .

Anwar/Father Nuri: Amen!

****

SCENE THREE

It is morning time. Anwar is tending the shrine. Father Nuri enters the stage carrying his basket of berries and fruit. He places the basket on the floor under the tree and walks to centre stage. He looks out over the auditorium as if surveying the landscape. Anwar comes over to join him.

Father Nuri: Out there, my son, are birds that sing sweetly, as if to tell us of their wonderful life.

Anwar: And they fly so swiftly as if to show us how wonderfully they were created.

Father Nuri: And the wind blows, sometimes gently, sometimes strong.

Anwar: As if the winds were there for the birds.

Father Nuri: And for us…the wind blows for us, my son. We are, after all, the highest of all our Lord's creatures.

Anwar: How could I forget, Father? Forgive me.

Father Nuri: You have already been forgiven. (*Anwar bows his head. Father Nuri remains staring out into the distance. He suddenly hears the sound of whistling*) What is this – birds whistling as humans do?

Anwar: Or humans as do birds?

Father Nuri: If it is a pilgrim then this pilgrim sounds jolly.

Anwar: And a jolly pilgrim has little use for a blessing.

Father Nuri: And so why disturb us?

Anwar: Another test, perhaps?

Father Nuri: Our Lord does test us much these past few days – does he not have mercy also?

Anwar: A custodian's work is never done.

Father Nuri: And faith must show no holes, my son.

Nassa appears on stage, walking casually, looking jolly and whistling.

Father Nuri: (*surprised*) Another Judas returns!

Anwar: He has not hanged himself.

Father Nuri: (*calling to Nassa as he approaches*) There is no place for you here!

Anwar: There is no room for you here!

Nassa: I desire neither your place nor your room.

Father Nuri: Then why do you return, creeping like a fox?

Nassa: *(smiling broadly)* Because this fox forgot his cap.

Anwar: Cap?

Nassa: For my head.

Anwar: Yes, I know what it's for – but what is it doing here?

Nassa: Waiting for my head! *(he goes into the hut and emerges shortly with a cap on his head)*

Anwar: I saw no cap in there.

Father Nuri: Nor I.

Nassa: I cannot be held responsible for your lack of perception - those with eyes shall see.

Father Nuri: It is trickery again!

Anwar: Once a charlatan, always a charlatan. That's what Father taught me.

Nassa walks over to the shrine and proceeds to pray in silence.

Father Nuri: What does he do now?

Anwar: It seems as if he prays.

Father Nuri: Bah, nonsense! He is trying to trick us once more.

Anwar: How so?

Father Nuri: By outward display of devotion.

Anwar: Yes, of course. How easy it is to see that his prayer is empty *(both Anwar and Father Nuri watch keenly as Nassa continues praying. When he's finished, Nassa walks over to both men)*

Nassa: Now I say goodbye.

Anwar: *(haughtily)* Goodbye.

Father Nuri: Enough of your empty rituals, they do not fool us. You are a cheat.

Nassa: I did not come to cheat.

Anwar: Your prayer meant nothing.

Nassa: No?

Anwar: It was an empty vessel, devoid of sincerity. It was a ritual done as habit. Rituals like that can be done a thousand times over without bringing benefit.

Father Nuri: You are merely trying to play the game of religion. It has no place in your heart.

Nassa: *(smiling)* Thank you. You have shown me many things.

Father Nuri: You are full of talk.

Nassa: Really?

Father Nuri: And you still have much to learn.

Anwar: From what I can see you are unlikely to ever be free of your chief feature of foolishness and idiocy.

Nassa: Not unlike the both of you, who are free of your chief features *(Anwar and Father Nuri nod in agreement).* Not unlike our Custodian here whose chief feature used to be greed.

Anwar: That is so.

Nassa: And now he passionately follows the path of generosity.

Anwar: *(feeling proud)* True.

Nassa: Yet does he not know that the greed for generosity is still greed? To have a greed for something good does not cancel out the fact that it is still a greed.

Anwar: You talk in riddles.

Father Nuri: Is this more of your lunatic talk?

Nassa: To do good works in the eyes of man is a greed for things of this world, not of true service. True generosity is free of the greed for personal gain; it is when the left hand knows not what the right hand does *(Anwar stutters and mumbles but has nothing to say).*

Father Nuri: Your words carry no weight around here.

Nassa: Not in the face of your vanity, they don't.

Father Nuri: *(affronted)* Meaning what?

Nassa: Meaning that the man whose chief feature used to be vanity still suffers from the greatest vanity.

Father Nuri: *(showing signs of anger)* How can you say that! You are a man of no spiritual insight.

Nassa: It doesn't take spiritual insight to recognise that it was your existing vanity which proclaimed your past vanity to be the worst sin of them all.

Father Nuri: *(protesting)* But it *was* the worst!

Nassa: *(bowing)* Voila! Now I have my cap I must leave you two most entertaining gentlemen *(Father Nuri and Anwar are huffing and puffing and making noises)*. I have to see a man about a donkey. Goodbye! *(Nassa exits)*

Father Nuri: *(shaking his head)* Has to see a man about a donkey – a true lunatic! This man is a fool, is he not, Anwar?

Anwar: *(quietly)* I suppose so *(Father Nuri looks at him)*.

Both men remain silent, looking out across the auditorium into the distance once again.

****

SCENE FOUR

It is night time. There is a full moon. Both men are standing at centre-stage – as if they haven't moved – looking up into the night sky. Stars are in the sky. Both men are illuminated by the glow of the full moon and are easily visible.

Father Nuri: The stars are in their glory tonight.

Anwar: Indeed.

Father Nuri: It surely is a wonderful creation. And to think that we are servants to such a thing.

Anwar: It really is beyond me.

Father Nuri: Me too

Both men look at each other, and then return their gaze to the stars.

Anwar: Father Nuri?

Father Nuri: Yes?

Anwar: Is sinning such a bad thing?

Father Nuri: No, not really. I think when it comes down to it we're all sinners – and it's no bad thing.

Anwar: Unless you're a big bad sinner.

Father Nuri: *(nodding)* Yes, unless you're a big bad sinner.

Anwar: Is it possible to be completely free of human faults?

Father Nuri: It must be, otherwise I'd lose my faith.

Anwar: But it's harder than we can possibly imagine, isn't it?

Father Nuri: I feel it is *(sighs)*

Anwar: Father?

Father Nuri: My son?

Anwar: I think there's something I should confess.

Father Nuri: Now's a good time.

Anwar: I served you many years at your shrine.

Father Nuri: You did.

Anwar: And I served upon you and all your needs.

Father Nuri: That you did.

Anwar: And you taught me much.

Father Nuri: Lord be praised.

Anwar: Then came the time when I had to leave you.

Father Nuri: I felt it was time for you to go your own way in the world.

Anwar: And so I left you and travelled upon the donkey that you gave to me.

Father Nuri: It was a donkey donated as a gift. Yes, it was a faithful creature.

Anwar: I travelled for many months, far and wide, living in constant austerity.

Father Nuri: It is our way.

Anwar: It was a hard time. I meditated much. Often I would gaze at the stars for guidance and inspiration *(both men look up at the stars)*…yet answers came not *(both men lower their heads)*.

Father Nuri: Sometimes the divine channel gets blocked. I fear the Lord's plumber is grossly over-worked.

Anwar: Whatever nourishment I obtained was from kindly strangers and I always shared it with my faithful donkey; she became my most trusted and loyal companion.

Father Nuri: I can understand how that may be.

Anwar: Yet times became harder; the travelling became more exhausting and my donkey grew weak. Eventually she could go no further and fell on the spot and quietly died. I was grief stricken.

Father Nuri: She did perform her duty well. She'll be rewarded.

Anwar: Her loyalty was beyond doubt; she had carried me forth without complaint or concern for herself.

Father Nuri: True servitude.

Anwar: I was so grieved that after burying her I could not move myself from her grave. I spent days without food or water. I even thought my own end days were approaching…until…

Father Nuri: A miracle?

Anwar: Not quite. A party of passing pilgrims spotted me.

Father Nuri: And they fed you?

Anwar: Honourably so. They saw my state and immediately believed that such sincere display of grief must surely prove that the grave belonged to a saint of high rank.

Father Nuri: And you did not deny it?

Anwar: And destroy their new arousal of faith? How could I?

Father Nuri: Yes, I see, the Lord's work is first.

Anwar: They left gifts and soon spread the word that here lay the grave of a great and noble saint. Before long I was flocked by eager pilgrims seeking blessings. Larger offerings were made and soon a tomb was erected.

Father Nuri: Son, where is this tomb of our donkey?

Anwar: *(pointing over his shoulder)* Behind us.

Father Nuri: Ah…*(Both men go quiet)*

Anwar: What can I say, Father?

Father Nuri: Say nothing *(pause)*…Anwar, my son?

Anwar: Yes, Father Nuri?

Father Nuri: You remember that shrine of mine where you served for so many long years?

Anwar: How could I forget, it was such a spiritual place for me - a model shrine.

Father Nuri: Don't rush to honour it so quickly.

Anwar: Why so?

Father Nuri: For that shrine is the grave of my donkey also.

Anwar: *(shocked)* Ah… *(both men go silent)*

Father Nuri: I was given a donkey by my teacher too and was sent away. Like you I travelled until the donkey dropped. The rest is the same history as yours.

Anwar: I see…

Father Nuri: Strange how things turn out.

Anwar: Most strange.

Father Nuri: And who are we to interfere with the Lord's Great Plan?

Anwar: *(nodding)* Us being mere mortals.

Father Nuri: I suppose only the Lord knows what is in men's hearts.

Anwar: And if he looks into ours?

Both men look silently up at the stars again.

Father Nuri: May the Lord be forgiving to all that He sees.

Anwar/Father Nuri: *(in chorus)* Amen.

Both men continue to gaze out over the auditorium as the curtain falls.

THE END

Printed in Great Britain
by Amazon